Driven: A Career in Reverse

Driven: A Career in Reverse

Miles West

Dedicated to Matt

Table of Contents

Chapter 1   The Accidental Chauffeur · 1
Chapter 2   Fog and Fist Bumps· 5
Chapter 3   Parking Karma and Other Urban Myths· · · · · · · · · 10
Chapter 4   Silicon Valley After Dark· 13
Chapter 5   Bumper Cars for Adults· 17
Chapter 6   The Mission—Impossible · · · · · · · · · · · · · · · · · · · 23
Chapter 7   The Invisible Man· 27
Chapter 8   Presidio of Peculiarities · 31
Chapter 9   The Golden Gate Grifters · · · · · · · · · · · · · · · · · · · 34
Chapter 10 Back Seat Confessionals · · · · · · · · · · · · · · · · · · · 40
Chapter 11 Emotional Surge Pricing · · · · · · · · · · · · · · · · · · · 45
Chapter 12 Aretha, Billie, and Me· 49
Chapter 13 GPS and Me · 52
Chapter 14 The Hangover Express · 56
Chapter 15 The Ethical Slut's Guide to Rideshare Etiquette · · · · 62
Chapter 16 The Crosswalk Chronicles· · · · · · · · · · · · · · · · · · · 65
Chapter 17 Last Ride· 68

Reflections on the Road · 73

CHAPTER 1

The Accidental Chauffeur

IF YOU'D TOLD ME A year ago that I'd become San Francisco's least qualified tour guide, I'd have laughed you out of the room. Similarly, if you'd predicted my unceremonious firing by a man I had secretly dubbed "Little Hittler," I'd have assumed you were hallucinating. However, life, it seems, has a twisted sense of humor—not unlike those 'Merge' signs on highways, cheerfully suggesting that two lanes of caffeine-addled commuters should seamlessly blend into one harmonious river of traffic. As if ….

Mere weeks ago, Soulless & Associates (not its real name, but close enough) showed me the door. My vertically challenged boss, a despot with a Napoleon complex and a penchant for firing assistants whenever the company relocated them to the main office, had decided it was my turn to face the guillotine. It was his way of ensuring he had a fresh-faced victim for him to torment in his lair of misery and paper cuts. And there I was, his latest casualty in this twisted game of musical chairs, forced to merge into the unpredictable stream of the unemployed.

The day they showed me the door, I hailed a rideshare home, marinating in self-pity and the lingering stench of corporate oppression. My driver, a cheerful soul with the patience of a saint and the navigational skills of a homing pigeon, seemed suspiciously content for someone who spent their days fighting San Francisco traffic.

Rolling through the city's maze-like streets, I found myself oddly fascinated by his calm demeanor. It was like watching a Buddhist monk navigate a mosh pit.

"How long have you been driving?" I asked, aiming for casual but landing somewhere between desperate and manic.

He explained that he'd been at it for a year, renting his car from the company for $250 a week. "Just take it in monthly for servicing," he said, as if describing a particularly good deal on a timeshare in purgatory. I listened with the intensity of someone who'd just discovered a new religion, or at least a new way to pay rent.

In the weeks that followed, I morphed into the world's most persistent rideshare passenger. Each ride became an off-the-cuff job interview that I hadn't been invited to conduct. I peppered drivers with questions about hourly rates, passenger horror stories, and strange discoveries in their back seats. These poor souls probably thought they'd stumbled into some bizarre reality show: "So You Think You Can Drive a Rideshare?"

In the rearview mirror of my newly rented Chevy Trax, my reflection stared back at me with all the confidence of a substitute teacher on their first day—which is to say, none whatsoever. The bags under my eyes suggested I'd been storing small groceries there, while my forced smile reminded me of those photos they take of you on roller coasters just before the big drop. If this was what a budget midlife crisis looked like, I'd clearly gotten the markdown version.

I'd crafted a playlist for my new career, kicking off with Nancy Wilson's "You'd Be So Nice to Come Home To." My love for music would become my signature move, adapting to each passenger's mood. Looking back, I realize I was less creating ambiance and more scoring my own personal descent.

My first ride request pinged through, triggering a cocktail of excitement and terror that I imagine skydivers experience right before they jump. Or perhaps it was more akin to the feeling of realization that you've just hit "Reply All" on a company-wide email detailing exactly why your boss is a tyrannical gremlin.

The passenger, a young woman engrossed in her phone, climbed in wordlessly. A Postmates cyclist, hunched over his handlebars like a gargoyle with a death wish, shot through the intersection while texting, forcing me to swerve. The magnitude of my unpreparedness hit me like a runaway cable car. Who was I kidding? Until last week, my greatest vehicular achievement had been parallel parking within six feet of the curb. Now here I sat, a newly minted chauffeur to strangers, trying not to kill anyone on my first day. When I'd pictured my next career move, it certainly hadn't involved dodging kamikaze delivery bikers while questioning every life choice that had led me to this moment. I attempted conversation with all the grace of a giraffe on roller skates: "So, uh, how's your day going?"

She glanced up, seemingly surprised to find herself sharing space with another human. "Fine," she replied before diving back into the digital world, leaving me to wonder if I'd imagined our brief exchange. By some miracle, we arrived at our destination without incident, though I'm pretty sure I aged five years in those fifteen minutes.

That first night, I completed eight rides, each a crash course in San Francisco's unique brand of chaos. There was the tech bro pitching his app idea for "Rideshare, but for dogs," and the couple who argued the entire way about whether Mission or North Beach had better Italian food (North Beach, obviously). And who could forget the woman insisting on giving turn-by-turn directions even though I had a GPS, and she was, by her own admission, "a little tipsy"?

My body collapsed into bed that night, muscles screaming from hours hunched over the steering wheel like some kind of human question mark. I couldn't help but laugh at the absurdity of it all. I had gone from corporate drone to accidental chauffeur in the span of a few weeks, trading my ergonomic chair for a driver's seat with questionable lumbar support. If this was a midlife crisis, at least it promised to be an interesting one.

Looking back now, after thousands of rides and countless stories, I realize that getting fired was the best thing that could have happened to me. It forced me out of my comfortable corporate cocoon and into the wild, weird world of rideshare driving, where every day brought new adventures and fresh reminders that life rarely goes according to plan.

San Francisco has a way of reshaping you, much like how its fog reshapes the city's skyline each morning. One minute you're a respectable paper-pusher with benefits and a 401(k), the next you're debating the merits of various taco trucks with strangers in your back seat at 3 a.m. But maybe that's the point. Sometimes you need to get lost to find yourself, even if "lost" means circling the block for the third time looking for a parking spot.

In the end, those "Merge" signs had it all wrong. I'd spent years fighting to blend seamlessly into the corporate fast lane, only to discover that the most interesting moments happen in the spaces between lanes. Now, as part of the endless flow of San Francisco traffic rather than fighting against it, I'd found my own peculiar rhythm in the chaos.

So here I am, ready to take you on a journey. Because if my time as a rideshare driver taught me anything, it's that the best journeys are the ones you never see coming. Welcome to my life as a rideshare driver in San Francisco. Buckle up, dear reader. It's going to be one hell of a ride.

CHAPTER 2

Fog and Fist Bumps

IF SAN FRANCISCO WERE A person, it would be that eccentric aunt who shows up to family gatherings in unexpected outfits, complaining about the weather while insisting she wouldn't live anywhere else. It's a city that prides itself on being weird, yet somehow manages to make the bizarre feel routine. Much like those "Yield" signs scattered throughout the city—supposedly there to promote order but are just a passive-aggressive suggestion that everyone ignores anyway.

Two months into my new career as San Francisco's least qualified tour guide, I'd upgraded to my second rental car—a 2018 Chevy Malibu that smelled faintly of broken dreams and pine-scented air freshener. I was also getting more comfortable with the city's layout, relying less on GPS and more on my growing mental map of San Francisco's convoluted streets.

It was on one particularly foggy morning that I encountered what I now call the "Inquisition on Wheels." The fog had rolled in thick and heavy, wrapping the city in its familiar gray embrace. I picked up a passenger outside one of those tech companies that always seems to be in the news for violating our privacy in new and exciting ways.

As soon as he got in, the questions started, refusing to yield to any notion of personal space or privacy.

"So, how long have you been driving?" he asked, his fingers already twitching towards his phone, no doubt ready to take notes

"About two months," I replied, hoping my tone would discourage further inquiry.

"And what did you do before this?" he pressed on, undeterred by my lack of enthusiasm.

I briefly considered inventing an elaborate backstory but settled for, "I worked in an office," I said, hoping the banality would bore him into silence.

No such luck. For the next twenty minutes, as we wound through fog-shrouded streets, he interrogated me about everything from my hourly rate to my thoughts on the gig economy. By the time I dropped him off, I felt less like a driver and more like a contestant on a particularly tedious game show.

I merged back into traffic, contemplating my newfound role in the universe's grand comedy. Just months ago, I'd been that insufferable passenger perched in the back seat, peppering every driver with questions about their career choices, hourly rates, and deepest regrets. Now karma had caught up with me like an unpaid parking ticket. Here I sat on the other side of the inquisition, fielding the same tedious questions I'd once lobbed at unsuspecting drivers. The universe, it seemed, had a peculiar sense of humor and an excellent memory for past transgressions.

Another evening, as the fog took a breather, I found myself hosting an impromptu social hour in my car. Three strangers, brought together by the algorithmic gods of ridesharing, engaged in conversation that soared past the usual small talk about the weather (foggy) and housing prices (astronomical) into the rarefied air of genuine connection. For a moment, I allowed myself to imagine a future where we'd gather for brunch, sharing inside jokes about this very ride. "Remember when we all met in that Nissan Altima?" we'd chortle, clinking our overpriced mimosas.

On a night when the city wore its fog like a comfort blanket, I welcomed aboard a woman who ran an AI company. We merged onto the 101 and she started sharing stories about interviewing coders, speaking about artificial intelligence with the casualness of someone discussing their grocery list. I nodded, trying to hide the fact that my most significant accomplishment that day had been successfully matching my socks. Here I was, a man who considered making his bed a herculean task, chauffeuring around someone who was literally programming our future overlords. I made a mental note to be extra nice to Siri from now on, just in case.

Our tête-à-tête was interrupted by the ping of another ride request. When we pulled up to a bar in Redwood City that looked like it had been decorated exclusively with items found in a dumpster, I spotted two men who appeared to have been poured directly out of the establishment's least sanitary glass.

"Perhaps," I suggested to my back seat CEO, employing all the tact of a bull in a China shop, "you'd be more comfortable moving to the front. These guys look like a hot mess."

She agreed, and we soon found ourselves subjected to a duet of slurred come-ons and off-color remarks that would make a sailor blush. I've heard more charming mating calls from rutting elk.

After dropping off our unwanted Shakespeare-in-the-gutter performers, my passenger exhaled a sigh of relief that could have powered a small wind farm. "Thank you," she said., "Moving to the front was good idea."

We bonded over the shared trauma, and I found myself confessing my literary ambitions. "I'm writing a book," I announced. "I'm calling it 'Driven.' It's about... well, this." I gestured vaguely at what just occurred.

She loved it, because of course she did. She was probably already calculating how to turn it into an AI-powered interactive experience. "You should have it ready in eight to sixteen months," she declared, with the assurance of someone used to bending reality to her will.

That was five years ago. If my book were a child, it would be starting kindergarten by now, probably already coding its own AI on the playground. But here I am, finally putting words to paper, proving that it's never too late to turn your life into a cautionary tale—or, in my case, a collection of them.

My next passenger—a sleep study patient with a penchant for fist bumping—truly tested my ability to maintain a straight face. I pulled up to a nondescript building to find him standing there, clutching a pillow like a life preserver. His fist shot out toward me, and for a moment, I thought I was about to become the victim of the world's drowsiest carjacking.

"Are you okay?" I asked, perplexed. "I used to be a rideshare driver," he explained, words slightly slurred from what I hoped was fatigue. "We always fist-bumped at the start of a ride."

The road stretched ahead while my passenger shared his sleep lab results with surprising cheerfulness. "They told me I stopped breathing thirty-seven times an hour," he said as casually as if he were discussing the weather. "Apparently, that's not great."

I nodded sympathetically, all the while thinking that maybe I should be the one in a sleep study. The engine hummed while we snaked through the murky, half-lit streets, the soulful voice of Aretha Franklin spilled from the speakers, as if she, too, was stuck in traffic and just trying to get home. Nothing like a little "R-E-S-P-E-C-T" to soundtrack your descent into madness, I thought.

We were cruising down Van Ness when a cyclist appeared from nowhere, swerving between lanes. I slammed on the brakes; grateful

I'd upgraded from the Chevy Trax with its questionable stopping power.

When I dropped him off at his apartment, pillow in hand, I marveled at the absurdity of it all. In this journey through the Bay Area's ever-changing landscape, sometimes the most important skill was knowing when to yield, and when to forge ahead, no matter what obstacles the road might could throw in your path. After all, in San Francisco, yielding wasn't just a suggestion—it was an art form, one that I was slowly mastering with each bizarre ride fare and fist bump. Because following your own path isn't just acceptable—it's practically mandatory.

CHAPTER 3

Parking Karma and Other Urban Myths

IF THERE'S ONE THING SAN Francisco has taught me, it's that parking karma works in mysterious ways. I first noticed this one night at Philz Coffee, watching a regular chant, "Isis, Isis, full of grace, help me find a parking space." At the time, I laughed. Six months later, I found myself muttering the same incantation. When you spend enough time roaming San Francisco's streets looking for parking, you learn that it's about who owns the right to occupy this city.

While most people measured their status in square footage and stock options, I measured mine in parking spots. In Pacific Heights, valets gave me the side-eye as I idled near their carefully guarded spaces. In the Financial District, I learned which taco trucks were worth the inevitable parking ticket. Each neighborhood had its own unwritten rules, its own hierarchy of who belonged where.

While Etta Jones's "Don't Go to Strangers" crooned about the beauty of holding close what you cherish, I picked up a man in Marin County, in one of those quaint, picturesque towns just north of the Golden Gate Bridge, where the air smells of money and entitlement. He was fresh off a construction job, covered in a fine layer of dust that probably cost more than my monthly rent.

The road carried us while Etta played softly through the speakers and he told me about his latest project—a client who'd bought the house next door to his mansion, not to live in, not to rent out, but solely to tear it down for a better view. Two million dollars for an unobstructed vista of the bay. In a city where people lived in their cars because they couldn't afford rent, someone was demolishing a perfectly good house to improve their sightline.

The same client's wife, not content with her multimillion-dollar abode, had the wooden floors replaced five times within that year. Each time, a different exotic hardwood failed to fill whatever void she was trying to cover. I thought about all the places that wood could have housed people instead of briefly satisfying one woman's restless desire for perfection.

These displays of excess felt particularly jarring during my battle with Haven, the company that managed my first rental car. When the Chevy Trax they'd assigned me developed brake issues on the first day, I entered a bureaucratic maze that made Kafka look optimistic. The rideshare company told me to call Haven. Haven directed me to their emergency line. The emergency line insisted I needed to talk to the dealership. Meanwhile, I was driving up and down San Francisco's hills in a car that stopped about as reliably as a politician's promises.

Haven eventually denied the repairs and retrieved their rolling death trap without informing me or my rideshare company, who continued charging me $250 a week for a car I no longer possessed. For two months, I was trapped between two corporations playing hot potato with my livelihood. It wasn't until I took to Twitter with my story that anything changed. What weeks of phone calls couldn't accomplish, 24 hours of social media shaming managed beautifully.

During this time, I picked up a former lawyer for one of these rideshare companies. He could only request rides through his wife's account, having been banned after some corporate falling out.

Between the brief stretches when he wasn't checking his phone, he shared insights about how these companies operated. "They only handle the catastrophic stuff—kidnappings, carjackings, police investigations. Everything else? They ignore it until it becomes a PR problem."

His words illuminated something I'd been sensing but couldn't articulate. In San Francisco, from parking spots to basic safety, everything was a commodity. Your right to occupy space, your right to safe working conditions, your right to simply exist in the city—it all depended on your position in an invisible hierarchy.

At one point, I found myself in Pacific Heights again, circling for a spot while a line of Teslas occupied prime spaces in front of a luxury boutique. A parking attendant watched me with the same expression I'd seen on bouncers at exclusive clubs. The message was clear: some people belonged here, and others didn't.

Looking back, I realize that parking karma wasn't really about parking at all. It was about belonging, about who gets to claim space in a city increasingly divided between those who can casually demolish multimillion-dollar homes and those who sleep in their cars. Whether you're searching for a parking spot or fighting with a soulless corporation over basic safety, you're really asking the same question: Do I have the right to be here?

In the end, I learned that sometimes the only way to claim your space is to make enough noise that they can't ignore you anymore. It might not help you find a parking spot, but it might just keep your brakes functional.

CHAPTER 4

Silicon Valley After Dark

GUIDING MY RENTED NISSAN MAXIMA onto the 101, I watched the "Two-Way Traffic" sign emerge from the fog. It felt fitting for a city constantly in flux between innovation and burnout, between dreams and disillusionment. Much like my own fluctuating understanding of what exactly I was doing with my life.

My passengers tonight were three young tech bros, fresh from what they called a "coding marathon" at their startup. Their animated chatter about disrupting the bitcoin industry with blockchain technology made me feel like I'd stumbled into a live taping of *Silicon Valley*, minus the self-awareness.

"Hey, driver," one called out. "Can you crank up the AC? It's hotter than our server room in here."

I complied, adjusting the temperature as we cruised past Stanford University. The cool air filled the car, carrying with it the faint scent of privilege and energy drinks. Each tech campus we passed was less a corporate office and more a miniature city, complete with its own transit system of primary-colored bicycles scattered like toys left behind by giant children. Between the buildings, manicured lawns hosted what looked like adult playgrounds. I spotted a volleyball court, a T-rex skeleton (because why not?), and what appeared to be a spiral slide emerging from a second-story window.

Facebook's Menlo Park headquarters loomed ahead, a massive hangar-like structure with an actual park on its roof. A giant thumb stuck out of the ground near the entrance—the physical manifestation of the "Like" button, or perhaps just Silicon Valley's way of hitchhiking to the future.

These corporate Disneylands were built to keep employees in a perpetual state of collegiate bliss, as if free snacks and foosball tables could compensate for the soul-crushing reality of spending your waking hours optimizing screen-scraping data. Traffic crept along, and the irony hit me like a Muni bus on a narrow street. Here we were, surrounded by companies dedicated to "disrupting" everything from dog-walking to dental floss, yet we were stuck in the same old dance of rush hour—or as I came to think of it, "rush to wait."

The playlist shifted to The Weeknd, his moody R&B a fitting soundtrack for the valley at night. We passed the illuminated signs of tech giants: Google, Apple, Oracle—each one a beacon of innovation or harbinger of doom, depending on who you asked.

After dropping off my startup founders, I picked up a group of aging rockers from a dimly lit dive bar. Their leather jackets and faded band T-shirts were a throwback to a time before Silicon Valley became synonymous with coding and venture capital. They regaled me with stories of their glory days, when they'd opened for Guns N' Roses and nearly signed with a major label. Now they were playing small gigs in bars, holding onto their dreams with the same tenacity as the tech bros, just with more tattoos and less venture capital.

The juxtaposition wasn't lost on me. In the span of an hour, I'd ferried both the future and the past of Silicon Valley. Both groups driven toward a version of success that seemed to grow more elusive with each passing year, while I navigated between them in my rented car, part of the invisible army that kept the valley running after dark.

A group of Google engineers piled into my car, their conversation an exotic blend of technical jargon and workplace gossip. Through the suburban streets of Mountain View, I found myself eavesdropping on a world I barely understood.

"Did you hear about the new project in Building 43?" one asked quietly. "It's not just AI. It's next-level stuff. We're talking about revolutionizing the entire industry."

"Sometimes I wonder if we're really making a difference," another sighed. "Or if we're just creating more ways for people to waste time on their phones."

The car fell silent, the weight of his words hanging in the air. Then, as if on cue, all their phones pinged simultaneously with what I could only assume was a work-related notification. The moment of existential doubt vanished as quickly as it had appeared.

I glanced at my phone, noting that I was just $50 away from that day's goal. Maybe I wasn't changing the world or making millions, but I was making my way on my own terms. Through the dimly lit streets of Silicon Valley, life flowed like two-way traffic before me. The bright-eyed optimism of the young techies, their heads filled with dreams of disruption and billion-dollar IPOs, streamed one direction. In the opposing lane, the world-weary wisdom of aging rockers, their glory days fading like old concert tees.

Another ping brought a bleary-eyed coder, fresh from a 2 a.m. coding session. We were all just cogs in Silicon Valley's machine, I realized. The engineers building the future, the drivers ferrying them around, the musicians providing the soundtrack—each of us playing our part in this strange ecosystem. The only difference was that some of us could afford to buy houses here, while others could barely afford to rent the cars we used to serve them.

My headlights carved through the darkness while I finally understood—Silicon Valley after dark wasn't just a place or a time—it was a state of mind. A liminal space where the glossy promise of tech culture met the gritty reality of those who served it. Where dreams of disruption collided with the basic need to make rent. Where innovation meant different things to different people: for some, it was developing AI that could change the world; for others, like me, it was finding new ways to survive in a world that seemed increasingly designed to exclude us.

Maybe that's why I felt most at home during these night shifts. In the darkness, the valley's hierarchies blurred. Tech moguls and gig workers, coders and musicians—we were all just navigating our own version of the future.

CHAPTER 5

Bumper Cars for Adults

IF YOU'RE EVER FEELING TOO good about humanity, try driving for a rideshare service on a Friday night in San Francisco. It's a special kind of purgatory where the city's streets transform into a giant pinball machine, with cars ricocheting between construction zones and confused tourists.

I quickly learned there are two types of people in this world: those who see traffic laws as absolute and those who see them as mere suggestions. How people drive often mirrors how they behave online, hidden behind the anonymity of their license plates, revealing their true nature when they think no one's watching.

One Friday night, I was piloting my latest rental car, a vehicle that protested every left turn with an unsettling groan, and I spotted four mid-sized cars bumper to bumper on the overpass near Berkeley. The drivers stood by their hoods, exchanging information with surprising calmness. The only damage appeared to be mental, as evidenced by their choice to block two lanes of traffic instead of pulling off to safety.

Rounding a corner onto one of Oakland's pockmarked streets, a mysterious pothole appeared out of nowhere, perfectly positioned to meet my tire. I was reminded that life rarely comes with warning signs, and I could have used one before starting this gig—preferably flashing "Abandon All Hope, Ye Who Enter Here."

My passenger, a middle-aged man clutching his side, sprawled across the back seat alternating between groans and rapid-fire directions to the hospital. "Gallstones," he managed between pained breaths. "Twelfth time this year... not great."

I nodded sympathetically, wondering if I should be the one seeking medical attention. After all, I was the one hallucinating about warning signs on every corner. Perhaps this job had finally driven me to madness, and I was actually in a padded cell somewhere, imagining I was a rideshare driver in the world's most ridiculous city.

Over time, I became an unwitting confidant, a mobile therapist for the teched and perplexed. People would climb into my car as strangers and leave an hour later having shared their deepest secrets, their wildest dreams, and occasionally, their lunch.

Take the Indian couple I picked up from SFO, headed to wine country to celebrate completing a big project. They decided on a whim to stop in San Francisco first, and somehow, I ended up not just their driver but their impromptu tour guide and dinner companion. At Perry's on the Embarcadero—a place I used to frequent in my former life when it was on Union Street. We sat under the twinkling Bay Lights installation, sharing Cobb salads and stories, and I realized this job was giving me something my corporate gig never had—genuine human connection.

Then there was the time I picked up two brothers taking their wheelchair-bound grandmother to see Black Panther. It was the boys' fifth time and their grandmother's first. While they wheeled her into the theater, you could feel the pride radiating from them. This wasn't just a superhero movie; it was a chance to share something monumental, a reflection of their own strength and heritage on the big screen. For their grandmother, it was a moment of history, watching her grandsons witness the rise of a hero that looked like them, a king who shared their skin and culture. The excitement in the air wasn't just for the action movie, but for the sense of belonging that had been long overdue.

However, I've also had my fair share of vehicular misadventures in this job. There was the time a Hummer rear-ended me at an IHOP, crushing my trunk like it was made of papier-mâché. I half expected a burst of confetti and a sign saying, "Congratulations! You've been Punk'd!" to pop out.

Then there was the Chevy Trax with brakes as slippery as a buttered floor. Driving that car was like trying to stop a greased pig on an ice rink. Another time, another car, I got in and started driving, only to notice a whistling sound coming from the smashed-in quarter rear window.

The crown jewel of my automotive misfortunes arrived one weekend morning when I approached the driver's side door with my usual pre-coffee stupor, key poised, only to find the door had apparently decided to become one with the rest of the car in some sort of metal origami experiment gone horribly wrong. The entire side was sideswiped, tires flat, door crumpled, completely totaled.

Of course, this happened on a weekend, when the car rental was closed, and I was in a street sweeping spot every Monday from 7 a.m. – 9 a.m. So I set my alarm for 7 a.m., determined to deal with it before the street cleaners arrived with their ritualistic Monday morning ticket-writing ceremony. But when I arrive at my car at 7:02 a.m., I found myself face-to-face with a parking enforcer who looked like he'd been weaned on lemons and a tow truck driver who looked like he'd seen this movie before.

"My car's totaled," I explained, gesturing at the mechanical carnage. "I just need two hours until the rental hub opens." At which point I will get to pay a $1000 deductible for the crash after having just lost an entire day's wage because of a hit-and-run. Where else can I work where I wake up owing money and do they have free coffee?

The parking enforcer glared at me while the tow truck driver—perhaps recognizing a kindred spirit in automotive tragedy—intervened on my behalf and explained the car was totaled. The enforcer finally backed down, but not before giving me a look that suggested I'd somehow violated not just parking regulations, but the entire construct of the laws of physics.

And then there was my beloved Malibu. Ah, the Malibu. If my rental cars were a dating history, the Malibu was the one that got away—or more accurately, the one I backed directly into a random pole in a parking lot. It was less a meet-cute and more a meet-crunch, ending with a $500 deductible and my dignity crumpled like a used paper cup. The pole, I should mention, was completely unharmed and probably still stands there today, waiting for its next victim. I imagine it has quite the collection of paint samples from various rideshare vehicles by now.

Let's not forget the car that got towed on Christmas Eve (apparently not a holiday in the San Francisco parking world) while I was delivering presents. "Ho, ho, hold on, where's my car?" Getting a $70 ticket was one thing, but the $500 to get it out of impound is what hurt the most. I went through ten cars in two years driving a rideshare. Strangely, I never had issues with my personal vehicles. Then again, I never drove them 14 hours a day in a city where traffic laws seem optional.

But the pièce de résistance was the baseball bat chase. One wrong turn in Marin County, and suddenly I was starring in a low-budget remake of *The Warriors*, being pursued by an angry driver wielding a Louisville Slugger as if he was trying to hit a home run with my headlights. After a frantic chase that would have impressed Steve

McQueen, I found refuge in a fire station, my heart racing faster than a tech CEO at a congressional hearing.

When I finally mustered the courage to leave, I realized I'd forgotten to sign off. As if the universe hadn't had enough fun at my expense, my phone pinged with a new ride request, which I reluctantly accepted, not wanting to risk a ding on my profile.

My rental car groaned along while I drove to pick up the new passenger when my phone rang. I hesitated, half-convinced it was my baseball bat-wielding pursuer calling to schedule a rematch. But it was just the new passenger, asking if I needed a witness for the crazy incident he'd apparently seen. I politely declined, assuring him I was fine, all while wondering if I'd somehow stumbled into the *Twilight Zone* of rideshare driving. Shaken and exhausted, I signed off and headed home that night, silently vowing to stick to less eventful routes. Still, as harrowing as the baseball bat chase was, my gallstone-laden passenger probably had it worse.

We pulled up to the emergency room and he tumbled out, a tangle of limbs and pained expressions. I couldn't help but wonder if his night's journey was about to get even bumpier while he staggered toward the entrance.

I merged back into traffic, The Black Keys filling the car as I headed toward my next pickup. Passing a crumpled Prius losing an argument with a light pole, I reflected on how in this city of innovation and inebriation, you learned to roll with the punches—and the potholes.

The city unfolded around me like a living, breathing entity. One moment I'd be cruising through the bustling streets of Chinatown, where the aroma of dim sum mingled with the scent of incense, and the next I'd be emerging into the Financial District, where sleek glass towers loomed over me, a stark contrast to the Victorian charm I just left behind.

Nina Simone's powerful vocals filled the car (my playlist was less "driver's choice" and more "soundtrack to a nervous breakdown") and I realized that being a rideshare driver in San Francisco was less about getting from point A to point B and more about the strange, wonderful, and often inexplicable journeys in between.

It was about the stories we tell ourselves and each other as we hurtle through life, hoping we're headed in the right direction. It was about navigating the dichotomy of a city constantly torn between its storied past and its tech-driven future. And sometimes, it was about just trying to make it through rush hour on Market Street without encountering a single jaywalker with a death wish.

CHAPTER 6

The Mission—Impossible

IF SAN FRANCISCO IS A three-ring circus, the Mission is center stage—a kaleidoscope of hipsters, taco trucks, and existential crises packed into a few vibrant square miles. Block after block, I guided my rented Nissan Altima through streets that seemed designed by someone with an aversion to left turns, I wondered if I'd stumbled into some peculiar social experiment. Life here seemed to move in only one direction: toward the absurd.

The Mission was a place where you were never more than 10 feet from someone rallying against something, probably the concept of regular soap or non-artisanal oxygen. It was a neighborhood where you could get a Frida Kahlo tattoo while drinking a craft beer and eating a locally sourced, gluten-free burrito without crossing the street.

I'd just picked up a group of passengers outside El Farolito, that temple of gastronomical endurance where burritos doubled as weightlifting equipment. We set off and the smell of sizzling carne asada mingled with the Nag Champa wafted in from a nearby head shop and overpowered by what I was pretty sure was locally sourced tear gas from a protest around the corner. The Mission never smelled the same way twice, but it always smelled interesting.

My passengers were embroiled in a heated debate about taqueria supremacy in the Mission.

"El Farolito's carnitas are clearly superior," one argued passionately.

"Are you kidding me? La Taqueria's carne asada is the stuff of legends," another countered.

A third chimed in, "You're both wrong. Cancún's al pastor is where it's at."

I kept quiet. In the Mission, taqueria loyalty is serious business. These weren't just restaurants they were arguing about—they were cultural battlegrounds, each order a vote for what version of the neighborhood would survive. I'd watched the evolution of these debates over months of late-night pickups, noticed how the arguments had shifted from purely about taste to increasingly about authenticity, about who had the right to claim expertise on Mission Mexican food.

We had to detour around an impromptu street festival, where a ukulele-wielding busker performed a surprisingly moving rendition of "Despacito." The crowd around him perfectly captured the Mission's current state: tech bros in Patagonia vests mingled with longtime residents in Raiders' jerseys, while tourists struggled to order bacon-wrapped hot dogs in broken Spanglish.

When we turned onto Valencia Street, my passengers moved on to discussing gentrification. It's a word that had begun to lose meaning through overuse, but driving these streets daily, I saw its effects in real time. The same corner where I'd picked up a grandmother heading to church last Sunday now hosted a line of people waiting for $7 toast. The parking lot where the food trucks used to gather had become a "modern artisanal marketplace."

"I miss the old Mission," one sighed, gazing at a row of freshly painted condos.

"The old Mission is still here," another countered. "You just have to know where to look."

They were both right. Every day, I watched the two Missions coexist, overlap, and occasionally collide. I'd pick up third-generation residents heading to their granddaughter's quinceañera, then circle back for tech workers bound for cold-brew coffee labs. My routes traced the borders between colorful, charming Victorian and Edwardian-style homes with detailed trim alongside glass encrusted contemporary condos with metal siding and orange accent panels. My car was a mobile observation post in the neighborhood's ongoing evolution.

We passed Dolores Park, where the scene could have been from any era of the neighborhood's history. Elderly Chinese ladies practiced tai chi near the tennis courts, their graceful movements a counterpoint to the chaotic energy of the drum circle near the bridge. On the grassy slope, hipsters attempted to teach a bemused homeless man how to use a selfie stick.

The park had become a kind of neutral zone, where all versions of the Mission coexisted, if not always comfortably. I'd watched families who'd lived here for generations share space with recent transplants, each group staking out their territory on the grass. The palm trees stood sentinel over it all, having witnessed every iteration of this neighborhood's identity.

My role in all this was complicated as a rideshare driver—I was both observer and participant in the changes. I ferried tech workers to their luxury apartments and longtime residents to their jobs, watched rent prices rise through the conversations in my back seat. I was part of the gig economy that was reshaping the city, yet I couldn't afford to live in the neighborhoods where I spent my days.

We finally arrived at their destination, a trendy coworking space that looked like it had been decorated by someone who exclusively shopped at Burning Man. They piled out, still arguing good-naturedly about the merits of various taquerias, and I realized this was what made the Mission special. It's a place of contradictions and coexistence, where tradition and innovation collided in unexpected and often beautiful ways.

Checking my phone for the next ride, I saw the pickup location was just a few blocks away. In the Mission, you never knew what's around the next corner. It could be a Michelin-starred restaurant or a hole-in-the-wall pupuseria that's been there for generations. It could be a cutting-edge art gallery or a dive bar where time seemed to have stopped sometime in the 1970s.

The neighborhood's changes weren't just about buildings or businesses—they were about people, about who gets to belong and who gets pushed out. Every fare told a different version of this story: the tech worker who loved the neighborhood's "character" but complained about the noise from the local bands, the longtime resident priced out of their childhood home, the restaurant worker commuting from Tracy because they couldn't afford to live where they worked.

In the quiet of the moving car, it occurred to me that we have no power over the flow of culture. Stories, traditions, dreams collide and mingle, flowing in all directions at once, creating something entirely unique, like the Mission—a neighborhood perpetually caught between what was and what would be.

CHAPTER 7

The Invisible Man

THERE'S ONLY ONE WAY TO survive as a rideshare driver in San Francisco: adapt or die. Or, in my case, pretend to be hard of hearing. At least, that's what I told myself when I decided to become the world's least convincing Helen Keller impersonator.

It started innocently enough. After the five hundredth passenger asked me if I liked driving for rideshare and what else I want to do for a living, something in me snapped.

These incessant interviews were grating enough, but when I realized I was only getting $3.75 for most of these short rides/interviews, it became unbearable. Later tax calculations revealed I made about $3 an hour after expenses. Three dollars. I could have made more money selling bootleg sourdough.

In a moment of desperation, I updated my profile to say, "Driver is hearing impaired." It was my personal "Do Not Enter" sign, a desperate attempt to ward off the endless small talk and entitled behavior. No more probing questions about my life story, no more unsolicited career advice, no more having to explain why I couldn't "just stop real quick" at seven different locations.

The irony, of course, hit me immediately when my very next passenger turned out to know sign language. When I dropped him off, he signed, "Thanks for the ride." I signed back, "You're welcome," thanking my old Boy Scout merit badge in ASL. It was a close call, but I managed to maintain my charade.

Under the streetlights of Chinatown, the scent of dim sum wafting through the air, guilt began to gnaw at me. My "hearing impairment" had started as a way to avoid small talk, but it had become a barrier between myself and the very human connections that occasionally made this job worthwhile.

The car wound through the city streets, my self-imposed silence a barrier between myself and the world, I couldn't help but ponder the irony of my situation. In a job that required constant communication, I had chosen to opt out, to retreat into my own quiet bubble. But in the days to come, as the miles ticked by and the unspoken stories of my passengers filled the air, I realized that sometimes the more you speak, the further you get from the truth. In the stillness of my feigned deafness, I was learning to listen in a whole new way.

The ethical implications weighed on me though. Was I mocking the deaf community? Was I taking advantage of people's kindness? Or was I simply trying to preserve my sanity in a job that demanded more social interaction than a daytime talk show host?

These thoughts plagued me as I picked up my next fare—a boisterous group of twenty-somethings headed to a party in the Marina. One of them spent the entire ride attempting to communicate with me through increasingly creative hand gestures. By the time we reached their destination, she had inadvertently insulted my mother, propositioned me, and ordered a pizza—or at least, that's what I gathered from her flailing arms.

Looking in the rearview mirror, I questioned who I'd become. A fraud, a phony, a fake deaf guy just trying to make it through another shift without losing his mind.

The universe, ever the comedian, decided to test my commitment to the bit. I picked up two women who, believing I couldn't hear them, spent the entire trip expressing views so racist they would have made Archie Bunker uncomfortable. I gripped the steering wheel tighter, my knuckles turning white, as I navigated through their sea of bigotry. In that moment, I would have given anything to actually be hard of hearing.

The final straw came on a foggy night in the Richmond District. My passenger, taking advantage of my supposed deafness, decided to use my back seat as her personal karaoke booth. Her rendition of Whitney Houston's "I Will Always Love You" was less *The Bodyguard* and more *The Texas Chainsaw Massacre*. When we got to the Bay Bridge, I seriously contemplated driving off it.

It was in that moment, somewhere between "And IIIIIII" and "will always love youuuuu," that I realized the absurdity of my situation. Here I was, a grown man pretending to be deaf to avoid small talk, now trapped in a mobile concert from hell.

After dropping off my tone-deaf passenger, I made a decision. I reached for my phone and turned off the "I am hard of hearing" notification. It was time to rejoin the world of the hearing, for better or worse. My self-imposed "Do Not Enter" sign had served its purpose, but now it was time to open the gates and let the cacophony of San Francisco back in.

However, my experience as a fake deaf driver had taught me a valuable lesson: sometimes, a little white lie could go a long way in preserving one's sanity. While I was no longer going to pretend to be hard of hearing, I needed a new strategy to mitigate the endless interviews. Thus, the "Distracted Driver" approach was born. When passengers started peppering me with questions about my life choices or thoughts on the gig economy, I'd politely interject with a simple phrase: "I'm sorry, I get distracted talking and driving at the same time."

To my surprise and delight, this tactic worked beautifully. Most passengers would nod understandingly, content to sit back and enjoy the ride in blissful silence. A few even commended me for my commitment to responsible driving. If only they knew the real reason behind my sudden reserve. In a city where everyone had a story to tell and a question to ask, sometimes you had to get creative with your defenses.

And so, with my "Distracted Driver" persona firmly in place, I merged back into the flow of San Francisco life, ready for whatever bizarre, beautiful, or bewildering experience awaited me around the next corner. The city stretched out before me, a labyrinth of stories waiting to be heard—but this time, I would be the one to decide when and how to listen.

CHAPTER 8

Presidio of Peculiarities

IF SAN FRANCISCO HAD A tagline, it would be "Steep Grade Ahead: Use Low Gear." Not just because of the infamous hills, but because everything here seems designed to keep you on your toes. One particularly odd day, I found myself playing an off-the-cuff game of airport bingo—SFO, OAK, and SJC, all in one shift. By the time I hit my third terminal, I was half-expecting to sprout wings and take off myself.

Once, I picked up two guys outside Baker Beach. They climbed in mid-conversation, already deep into the kind of debate that was just begging for an audience—something about how densely populated places lean left politically, while folks in wide-open spaces tend to vote right. The conversation reminded me of a TV segment I'd seen where scientists looked at brain scans of liberals and conservatives to compare their "fear centers." Conservative brains lit up like Christmas when shown certain images, while liberals' brains remained as calm as a meditation retreat.

Between stoplights, I started wondering: maybe being surrounded by other people all the time just makes you feel safer? All that noise and closeness either soothes you or numbs you. But the person with nothing around them but trees and distant horizons? No wonder they start seeing threats in the shadows. Left, right—maybe we're all just victims of our geography, reacting to brain wiring and where we happen to be standing.

On another day, as I wound my way through the Presidio, with its mysterious blend of military history and natural beauty, the city's chaos gave way to an eerie calm. The towering eucalyptus trees stood like silent sentinels, their branches creating a natural canopy that seemed to absorb all sound. The transition from urban jungle to this otherworldly oasis was jarring, as if I'd crossed some invisible boundary into a parallel universe.

I picked up three medical students, their conversation a mix of enthusiasm and gallows humor about rare genetic disorders.

"So then," one said, "we got to the part about rare genetic disorders, and I swear, it's like Mother Nature was having a bad day when she came up with some of these."

His companion nodded enthusiastically. "I know, right? Like that one where your body turns to bone if you so much as stub your toe. Can you imagine?"

Their conversation turned to mushrooms. One student shared his expertise: "What I heard is you gotta be in nature."

The experienced one replied, "Sometimes, and sometimes not. It depends on the trip. The thing is to not overthink it." The conversation drifted into caps versus stems ratios and different ingestion methods, with peanut butter emerging as the consensus choice.

"You know," the other chimed in, "I heard mushrooms can actually help with cluster headaches."

I nodded, pretending I wasn't imagining a world where stubbing your toe could turn you into a living statue. The "Steep Grade Ahead" sign suddenly felt like a metaphor for my sanity slipping away.

Then came the day of the three-legged dog trifecta. Within hours, I encountered three tri-pawed champions: a confident retriever in Berkeley, a lounging pit bull outside a Concord café, and a determined dachshund in Fremont, each one moving through the world with more grace than most humans I knew. By the third dog, I started wondering if the universe was trying to tell me something about adaptation, or if I'd just driven into the twilight zone.

Later that week, at a red light in San Jose, I watched a woman clinging to the hood of a white BMW, screaming "Stop the car!" as it disappeared over an overpass. In my rearview mirror, I caught my own expression: the blank stare of someone who'd been driving too long in a city that had long since abandoned the plot.

Even Halloween in the Castro—usually a reliable catalog of weirdness—managed to surprise me. A gender-swapped Beetlejuice and Lydia caught my eye, the woman inhabiting Beetlejuice's manic energy while her male companion captured Lydia's gothic melancholy perfectly. Their role reversal somehow felt more authentic than the original, which seemed exactly right for San Francisco.

Just a week after the courts declared rideshares as taxis, I got ticketed for using a taxi lane. The officer might as well have handed me a "Welcome to the Confusion" sign along with the citation. But that's San Francisco for you—a city where even the rules about breaking rules have rules.

Some nights, crossing these streets felt less like navigation and more like negotiation with chaos itself. But maybe that's what made it home. In a city where three-legged dogs roamed like omens and every traffic light held the potential for performance art, we were all just trying to make it to the other side with our stories intact.

CHAPTER 9

The Golden Gate Grifters

IF THERE'S ONE THING SAN Francisco excels at besides housing crises and sourdough bread, it's scams. The "No Stopping" sign caught my eye as I navigated through the city's streets, a fitting metaphor for the constant hustle unfolding around me. In a city where everyone's trying to get one over on someone else, stopping meant becoming a mark yourself. It's like a city-wide game of three-card monte, only instead of cards, we're playing with overpriced real estate and kombucha on tap.

It was nearing the end of another 14-hour shift, my eyes glazed over from staring at the road and my back aching from hours in the driver's seat. My phone pinged with a new ride request, because of course it did. The app didn't care that I'd been driving longer than most people slept. It was the Silicon Valley way—work until you drop, then order a rideshare to take you to the ER.

The pickup spot was in the Tenderloin, a neighborhood where even the pigeons looked like they carried switchblades. When I pulled up to the curb, a woman stumbled toward my car, carrying the distinct air of someone who had started drinking sometime around yesterday and was just now coming up for air.

She collapsed into the back seat, bringing with her the aroma of vodka and poor life choices. I started the ride, only to watch in horror as she promptly canceled it on her phone.

"Did you just cancel the ride?" I asked, trying to keep the weary desperation out of my voice.

"No, I did nothing," she replied with the confidence of a toddler denying they had eaten pudding when their face was covered in it.

I'd been duped by many things in my life—I once thought chocolate milk came from brown cows. I even briefly believed that kale chips were a satisfying snack. But the "cancel the ride" trick was amateur hour. Yet here I was, facing the reality that trust is a luxury I could no longer afford in this job.

"Sorry," I said, channeling my inner flight attendant. "No fare, no ride."

She huffed and puffed and threatened to blow my rating down, but eventually staggered out of the car. When I pulled away, she yelled after me, "Asshole!"

I wanted to yell back, "That's Mr. Asshole to you," but I'd learned that engaging with drunk people was like trying to reason with a squirrel—it's pointless, and you'll probably end up with rabies.

I'd been naive once, back when I first started driving. I used to believe in the shared economy's promise of connection, of strangers helping strangers navigate the city. But San Francisco had its own plans for my idealism. Each attempted scam chipped away at my trust, replacing it with a hypervigilance that exhausted me almost as much as the long hours behind the wheel.

While I navigated the treacherous waters of customer service, I quickly learned that a sense of entitlement was not limited to any one demographic. From tech bros who treated me like their personal chauffeur to socialites who seemed affronted by the very idea of sharing a ride, I encountered more than my fair share of passengers who seemed to view me as little more than an extension of their smartphone. It was a stark reminder that money and manners don't always go hand in hand.

But the grifters of San Francisco are nothing if not diverse. They come in all shapes, sizes, and levels of sobriety. There was the time I picked up two boys who had only ordered a ride for one person. They climbed into my car with exaggerated casualness.

"Hey, man," the older one said, his voice dripping with false innocence, "my little bro here is just gonna hop in with me. That cool?"

I looked at them in the rearview mirror. They stared back with the wide-eyed innocence of kids trying to sneak an extra cookie. I'd seen more convincing performances in middle school theater productions.

"Sure," I said, "as long as you update the ride to two passengers. The next request might be for two people, and you won't all fit."

Their faces fell faster than San Francisco property values during a tech bust. They huddled together, whispering furiously as if planning a heist instead of trying to save pocket change.

"Uh, we don't know how to do that," the older one said. "Can't you just let it slide?"

I considered explaining the economics of rideshare driving, how every dollar counted when you were essentially running a small business out of a rented car. I thought about launching into a lecture on ethics and fairness. But it was late, I was tired, and I had about as much desire to educate these two as I had to take up underwater basket weaving.

"Nope," I said, popping the "p" for emphasis. "Either update the ride or one of you can walk."

They updated the ride.

The irony wasn't lost on me. In a city built on "disruption" and "innovation," the most common scams were remarkably simple. Cancel the ride mid-trip. Claim your driver was drunk. Report a nonexistent accident. Each week brought a new variation on the same theme: how to get something for nothing in a city where everything cost too much.

These boys reminded me of another encounter with San Francisco's junior league of grifters. One evening, I had picked up four teenagers from a movie theater. When they exited at their stop, I noticed my charging cord had vanished—my small gesture of Silicon Valley hospitality gone with the wind.

I stepped out of the car, feeling every mile I'd driven that day. "Excuse me," I called out, my voice carrying the weariness of a substitute teacher on the last day before summer break. "I think you might have accidentally taken my charging cord."

They turned; faces arranged in masks of innocence that wouldn't have fooled a particularly trusting golden retriever. "Nope," said one, popping the "p" like he was auditioning for a bubble gum commercial. "Don't know what you're talking about."

I'd dealt with many things in this job—drunk passengers, back seat drivers, and people who thought their life story was so fascinating it needed to be shared in the span of a fifteen-minute ride. But teenage cord thieves? That was a new low.

In a moment of inspiration (or perhaps desperation), I pulled out my phone and made a show of dialing. "Hello, Rideshare? Yes, I need to report a stolen item. I'd like to charge the passengers' account and cancel their ability to use the service."

The transformation was immediate. The cord materialized as if by magic, pulled from a pocket with the reluctance of a child surrendering their Halloween candy.

"Oh, this cord?" said the ringleader, holding it out. "We were just, uh, keeping it safe for you."

I took the cord and left. Upon leaving, I couldn't help but shake my head. In a city brimming with tech billionaires and "disruptive" start-ups, the best these kids could come up with was swiping a charging cord? It was almost disappointing. I expected better from the next generation of San Francisco hustlers.

These small-time grifts felt almost quaint compared to the larger scams being run by the companies themselves. While passengers tried to dodge five-dollar fares, the rideshare companies were playing their own games with our livelihoods—manipulating surge pricing, changing pay structures without notice, treating basic safety concerns as optional upgrades.

I began to see how the constant hustle affected us all. Passengers trying to game the system because they couldn't afford the rides they needed to get to jobs that didn't pay enough. Drivers learning to distrust everyone because one scam could erase a day's earnings. Companies treating both groups as disposable data points in their quest for profitability.

But then again, maybe that was the real innovation—finding new ways to pull off the same old tricks. The night stretched ahead, full of more potential scams and schemes. But I was ready. After thousands of rides, I'd developed a sixth sense for bullshit, a finely tuned detector for the city's countless con artists. Let them try their worst—I was the Houdini of rideshare drivers, always one step ahead.

The city's fog rolled in, as I picked up my next passenger—a man in a suit who immediately started complaining about surge pricing—I felt a familiar cynicism rising, then caught myself. When had I become so jaded? When had every interaction become a potential con to guard against? I realized that this constant state of vigilance was taking its toll not just on my patience but also on my very view of humanity.

I found myself second-guessing every compliment, scrutinizing every tip, suspecting an ulterior motive behind every friendly conversation. It was exhausting, this perpetual distrust. But in a job where letting your guard down could cost you your livelihood, what choice did I have?

As I cruised through the city streets, I wondered if this was the real price of being a rideshare driver in San Francisco. Not the long hours or the wear and tear on my bank account, but the gradual erosion of my faith in human nature. Was this hypervigilance protecting me, or was it robbing me of genuine connection?

CHAPTER 10

Back Seat Confessionals

IF MY RIDESHARE CAR WAS a temple, then I was the most overworked and underpaid high priest in San Francisco. I'd heard more secrets, fears, and existential crises in my back seat than a therapist's couch on a full moon Friday. My playlist, a carefully curated mix of Etta James and Billie Holiday, provided a soulful backdrop to the city's endless parade of human drama.

One memorable ride was a single mother, her voice a mixture of fury and despair as she railed against her ex-husband and the custody arrangement that had left her feeling like a weekend babysitter. Her words tumbled out like she'd been holding them back for years as we approached the Bay Bridge. I listened, nodding along sympathetically, while silently wondering if I should start charging by the hour.

"He's got this big house, this new wife," she spat, each word dripping with bitterness. "And our daughter... she chooses to live with him. Can you believe it?"

I found myself sharing a truth I'd never told another passenger. "When I was fourteen," I said, "my mom fell asleep at the wheel on Highway 4 in Byron. Middle of the afternoon, just drifted across the center line into a Mack truck. I was sitting in freshman biology when it happened." I paused, the familiar weight of the memory settled in.

"They had to use dental records to identify her. The newspaper photo showed a charred figure still gripping the steering wheel."

She stared right at me.

"Here's what I know now," I continued softly. "When your daughter graduates, when she falls in love, when she has her first child—those are the moments she'll want her mom there. No big fancy house or stepmother her own age can replace that. You're not losing her. You're just watching her grow up."

In the rearview mirror, I watched something shift in her expression—grief giving way to understanding. Sometimes it takes seeing your pain reflected in another's story to recognize your own truth: that being a mother isn't about where you live or what you own, but about being there when it matters most. Her tears subsided as she slowly realized the truth—that she had lost nothing.

Through the fog-laden streets, my own memories surfaced: my mom waking me each morning, sitting on the edge of my bed, running her fingers through my hair, humming softly until I stirred. No alarm clocks, no harsh voices—just that gentle transition from dreams to day. Even now, I can still feel her fingers in my hair, still hear that quiet humming. These are the moments that stay with you, that shape you, that no mansion or new wife could ever replace.

"You know," I said, surprising myself with my sudden eloquence, "I'd give anything to have one more conversation with my mom."

The woman fell silent, and I worried I'd overstepped. Great job, I thought to myself. But as I pulled up to her house, she leaned forward and said, "Thank you," her voice thick with emotion. She left a $20 tip and a five-star rating, but more importantly, she left with a glimmer of hope in her eyes.

For weeks after, I found myself wondering about her. Did she take my advice to heart? Did her relationship with her daughter improve?

Or did my words evaporate like morning fog as soon as she stepped out of my car?

The parade of confessions continued. Tech executives discussed corporate strategies in hushed tones, apparently forgetting that drivers have ears. I pretended not to listen while thinking how different their world was from mine. They debated acquisitions and IPOs while I calculated if I could afford both dinner and gas that night.

Once I picked up a father and son duo who were deep in conversation about the publishing world. The son, it turned out, was an aspiring author.

"Dad, I don't know," the son sighed. "Getting published seems impossible these days."

The father, who I later learned worked in publishing, chuckled. "You know, when I started, we didn't even have email. Now you've got agents on Twitter. Times change, but good stories always find a way."

Buildings blurred past as they debated traditional publishing versus self-publishing, I found myself fascinated. It was like eavesdropping on a master class in the literary world. When I dropped them off, the son turned to me with a grin. "Hey, if you ever write a book about your rideshare adventures, I bet it'd be a bestseller."

If only he knew.

I merged back into traffic, the familiar strains of Dinah Washington's "What a Difference a Day Makes" filling the car. Another ping, another ride request. Another confession waiting to be heard.

Perhaps the most poignant ride came from a man heading to physical therapy. I wrestled his wheelchair into my trunk—a task they definitely hadn't covered in rideshare orientation—while he eased himself into the passenger seat. The moment the door clicked shut, he began unspooling his saga with Social Security disability, each word heavy with the particular exhaustion that comes from fighting bureaucracy while healing bones.

"They denied me," he said, voice trembling with disbelief. "How can they deny someone with two broken legs?"

Mile after mile, he shared his story—a workplace accident, years of recovery, and now an endless paper chase through government offices. I listened, offering what comfort I could from my own journeys through that particular circle of hell, where hope goes to drown in triplicate forms.

"You know," I said, "the system is designed to wear you down. They deny everyone the first couple of times. You actually have to appeal around three times to finally get approved."

His eyes widened. "Three times?"

I nodded, feeling like some wise sage imparting ancient wisdom. "It's a marathon, not a sprint. But you'll get there."

While I watched him disappear through the hospital doors, I thought about how many times I'd been the last person someone spoke to before a moment that would change their life—whether it was walking into rehab, leaving a marriage, or starting over in a new city. These weren't just rides; they were thresholds between what was and what would be.

Late at night, when the city quieted and the fog rolled in thick enough to muffle even the most persistent thoughts, I'd sometimes find myself remembering these stories. The midnight confessions, the dawn revelations, the tears shed in rush hour traffic. Each one had worked its way into me, like water slowly reshaping stone. I hadn't asked to become San Francisco's unofficial keeper of secrets, but here I was, collecting fragments of lives like others collected souvenir magnets or concert tickets.

In a city obsessed with disruption, where every startup promised to revolutionize something, maybe there was something radical about simply bearing witness. About sitting in silence while someone pieced themselves back together in your back seat. About being the stranger who listened when even friends had grown tired of the same old stories.

I checked my phone for the next ride request, wondering what story waited around the corner. Because that's the thing about San Francisco—just when you think you've heard it all, someone climbs into your car and proves you wrong.

CHAPTER 11

Emotional Surge Pricing

IF SAN FRANCISCO'S ECONOMY WERE a person, it would be that friend who's always either flush with cash or begging you for bus fare—there's no in between. My newly rented Kia Optima wheezed its way up one of the city's infamous hills, and I felt the metaphor in every shuddering gear shift.

In the topsy-turvy world of rideshare driving, my earnings were as volatile as a tech startup's valuation. One moment I'd be raking in surge fares like a modern-day gold prospector, the next wondering if I should plan a career in panhandling. Such was the gig economy life—constantly in flux between innovation and burnout, dreams and disillusionment. Much like my own fluctuating understanding of what exactly I was doing with my life. The "No Standing" sign loomed before me, a reminder that in the gig economy, you were always one fare away from either feast or famine.

It was one of those rare sunny days that brought San Franciscans out of their fog-induced hibernation. My phone pinged incessantly with ride requests, the surge pricing icon flashing like a slot machine. A $12 trip would become $37, and drivers, hiding their glee, would nod sympathetically as passengers grumbled about the increased rates. It was capitalism in miniature: drivers cashing in, passengers complaining, and no one truly winning—except maybe the rideshare companies.

The constant financial uncertainty was taking its toll. I couldn't remember the last time I'd had a full night's sleep, my mind always racing with calculations—how many rides did I need to make rent? Could I afford to take a day off? What if my car broke down? The stress rode shotgun on every trip.

My relationships were suffering too. I'd missed my nephew's birthday party because I couldn't afford to turn down the surge pricing. My partner was starting to forget what I looked like without bags under my eyes. "You look like you need a vacation," they'd said during our last movie date. I couldn't argue—I did.

That night unfolded like a fever dream directed by Salvador Dali. I played therapist to a passenger convinced his studio apartment was a repurposed broom closet ("It's not the size," he insisted. "It's the lingering smell of roach bomb"), amateur sex educator to giggling twenty-somethings ("No, 'surge pricing' is not a euphemism"), and silent sanctuary to the hungover masses crawling their way to Sunday brunch. Each fare was a new adventure, a glimpse into lives so different from my own, yet connected by the shared experience of trying to make it in a city that seemed designed to break you.

But nothing could have prepared me for the El Cerrito Incident. I picked up a woman as part of a shared ride, and she immediately launched into a tirade about having to share the car with other passengers.

"I can't believe I have to do a line," she hissed. "Do you know who I am?"

I resisted the urge to reply with something sarcastic. Instead, I mustered my most diplomatic tone. "Ma'am, you chose the shared ride option. It's like a carpool."

She huffed. "I didn't choose this ride, my friend did. Why do I gotta be in this shitty car with these goddamned people?"

The tension in the car could have powered a small city. I would've frozen solid if I hadn't already been driving, so I did what any sane person would do: I kept my eyes on the road and pretended not to notice. Finally, mercifully, we reached her stop, and she bounced out without shutting the door.

Night crept on, painting the city map with surge pricing's seductive palette of red and orange. On nights like these, it was easy to get caught up in the frenzy, chasing high-paying rides like a gambler on a hot streak. But I'd learned to treat surge pricing the way locals treated the weather forecast—with deep suspicion and the knowledge that no matter what it promised, you'd probably end up cold and disappointed.

While refueling at a gas station during one of those rare moments when San Francisco wasn't actively trying to kill me, I spotted another rideshare driver across the way. He wore the same hollow-eyed, thousand-yard stare I'd been perfecting—that special blend of fatigue and mild trauma that comes from shepherding the drunk and entitled through the city's maze-like streets for fourteen hours straight.

"Rough night?" I called out.

He looked up, surprised, then nodded. "You know how it is. Chasing that surge like it's the Holy Grail."

We fell into easy conversation, swapping war stories about entitled passengers and impossible traffic. It was a relief to talk to someone who understood, who lived the same daily hustle. We traded tips on the best places to find rides, the cleanest public restrooms, the fastest routes during rush hour. For a moment, I felt a sense of camaraderie, a connection in this often-isolating job.

But the moment was fleeting. A ping on his phone, and he was off, chasing the next fare. I watched him go, feeling a mix of envy and resignation. We were all competitors, even as we faced the same struggles.

I picked up a college student at UC Berkeley once, headed to catch a flight at SFO. She had a large group of friends gathered around, waving goodbye like she was departing on some grand adventure rather than an ordinary flight. They were waving enthusiastically as she got in, and she waved back with a bittersweet smile. As soon as I pulled away, her face crumpled, and she began to cry softly. Now, if there's anything I know about the inside of a car, it's that it's the perfect place for a breakdown. Enclosed, private—just you, the driver, and a bunch of well-padded seats.

I switched on "Good Life" by Nancy Wilson, hoping the music might help her process whatever goodbye she was mourning. I knew loss myself, the kind you feel in your spine. The song washed over her and by the time we reached the airport, her eyes had cleared. She whispered "Thank you" as she disappeared into the terminal. Her dorm, her friends, her life in the Bay Area now just another part of her journey, etched into the rearview mirror.

Merging back into traffic one last time, I felt the familiar ache in my shoulders and that peculiar emptiness that comes from giving pieces of yourself to strangers all day. San Francisco has a way of keeping you in constant motion—stand still too long and the city moves on without you, leaving you behind like last week's trending topic or yesterday's unicorn startup.

When I drifted toward sleep that night, numbers still dancing behind my eyelids—surge rates, mileage, time logged—I thought about how we're all just trying to calculate our worth in a city that runs on algorithmic promises. But maybe the real surge wasn't in the pricing or the dopamine hits from five-star ratings. Maybe it was in those rare moments when the fog parted just enough to let us see each other clearly, if only for the length of a ride.

CHAPTER 12

Aretha, Billie, and Me

THE "SOUND WALL" SIGN CAUGHT my eye as I navigated onto the 101 late one night. It seemed fitting—in a city as loud as San Francisco, sometimes you need a barrier between yourself and the cacophony of urban life. For me, that barrier was sound itself: carefully curated playlists that served as both armor and bridge in my mobile confessional.

I got more comments on my music than anything else in my car. At first, I thought it was just passengers being polite, making small talk about whatever filled the silence. But over time, I realized my song choices were doing more than providing background noise— they were creating a soundtrack for the city's endless parade of human drama.

My musical arsenal wasn't random. Each selection was a calculated choice, an attempt to shape the energy in my car. Aretha Franklin's "Respect" for the tired service workers heading home after late shifts, her powerful voice a reminder of dignity in a city that often forgot about its essential workers. Billie Holiday's "Strange Fruit" for quiet early mornings when the fog wrapped around the city like a shroud, her haunting vocals echoing through empty streets.

When tech bros piled in after happy hour, I'd switch to something more contemporary—The Weeknd or Post Malone—music that let them feel comfortable while keeping them just calm enough not to throw up in my back seat. For the late-night hospital workers, it was usually Nina Simone, her voice carrying both strength and weariness, mirroring their own exhaustion.

One night, I picked up an elderly woman from the symphony. Her face still glowed with post-performance contentment, and in a moment of inspired genius (or perhaps temporary insanity), I put on some Pavarotti. Her face lit up as if I'd just handed her the keys to La Scala.

"Oh, Luciano!" she exclaimed, clasping her hands to her chest. And then, without warning, she began to sing along. Loudly. By the time I dropped her off, my ears were ringing, but her joy had made the temporary hearing loss worth it.

The city itself seemed to demand different soundtracks at different times. Dawn called for Chet Baker's trumpet soaring over the awakening streets. Rush hour needed the calming affect classical provided to keep my sanity intact while stuck in traffic. Late nights belonged to nu disco and neo soul, their electronic landscapes matching the city's neon-lit transformation.

The music became more than entertainment—it was my survival tool. When passengers tried to engage in conversations I didn't want to have, I could turn up Beethoven just enough to make casual chat difficult. When tension filled the car, some Sade could smooth things over. The right song at the right moment could deflate anger, ease awkwardness, or bridge cultural divides.

I remembered one particularly intense ride with a group of tech executives discussing layoffs in their company. They debated the fate of their employees while I quietly put on Sam Cooke's "A Change Is Gonna Come." The irony wasn't lost on anyone in the car, and the conversation shifted to more humane territory.

Life flowed like a complex symphony before me. The bright-eyed optimism of young techies, their heads filled with dreams of disruption and billion-dollar IPOs, called for one kind of music. The world-weary wisdom of aging musicians, their glory days fading like old concert tees, demanded another. If youth only knew, if age only could—the eternal refrain of the human condition playing out in the back seat of my car.

In those moments between rides, looking for my next passenger, I'd play my favorites—Lord Huron, Tori Amos, Erykah Badu, or Leon Bridges. Each song carried memories of past rides, past conversations, past lives briefly intersecting with mine. The music had become my diary, each track a timestamp of specific moments in my journey through the city's endless nights.

Through the music, I found ways to connect with passengers I might otherwise have nothing in common with. A shared appreciation for a jazz standard could bridge the gap between a venture capitalist and their driver. A mutual love for soul music could create unexpected moments of harmony in an otherwise discordant city.

I swung around another corner while my GPS announced another pickup, Billie Holiday's voice filling the car with tales of heartbreak and resilience. I realized that perhaps I had the best seat in the house for today's ongoing dramedy. Front row, center, with a steering wheel for an armrest and San Francisco in stereo.

CHAPTER 13

GPS and Me

MY RELATIONSHIP WITH GPS was like a bad rom-com: lots of miscommunication, wrong turns, and the occasional screaming match. The "Curve Ahead" sign flashed in my peripheral vision as my digital co-pilot cheerfully announced "recalculating" for the third time in ten minutes. I'd come to understand that "recalculating" was GPS-speak for "I have no idea where we are, but I'm too proud to admit it."

One day, as I drove, the robotic voice of my GPS broke through the silence, a digital reminder of my technological dependency. I guided my newly rented Ford Focus through the historic streets of Nob Hill, reflecting on my complicated relationship with this omniscient navigator.

It was a typical San Francisco afternoon—which is to say, it was anything but typical. The sun was playing hide and seek with the fog, and the streets were their usual chaos of tourists, tech workers, and what appeared to be a group of performance artists dressed as giant avocados.

I'd just picked up a passenger from one of those swanky hotels on California Street, a businessman from New York who seemed on the verge of a stress-induced aneurysm.

"How long until we get there?" he barked, barely looking up from his phone.

I glanced at the GPS. "About twenty minutes, traffic permitting."

He grunted, clearly dissatisfied I didn't bend the laws of physics to his will.

The GPS chimed in again. "In five hundred feet, turn right." I knew better. That particular right turn would take us directly into a one-way street—the wrong way. It wasn't the first time my digital copilot had tried to lead me astray, seemingly oblivious to the very concept of "Wrong Way" signs.

I thought back to all the times GPS had been both my savior and my nemesis. There was the night it had decided the fastest route to SFO was through what I was pretty sure was someone's backyard. Or the time it confidently directed me to drive off a pier and into the bay, as if I was auditioning for the next *Fast and Furious* movie.

But for every misstep, there were moments of brilliance. Like the time it navigated me through a maze of closed streets and construction zones, finding a path I never would have discovered on my own.

"Recalculating," the GPS announced again, apparently as confused by San Francisco's layout as I often was.

My passenger sighed heavily. "Do you know where you're going?" he asked, his tone suggesting he'd rather be piloting the car himself.

"Don't worry," I assured him. "I know this city like the back of my hand." It wasn't entirely a lie. After thousands of rides, I had developed an intimate knowledge of San Francisco's quirks and shortcuts. But in a city that seemed to reinvent itself every other week, sometimes even the back of my hand felt unfamiliar.

Through the tangle of San Francisco's streets, a Waymo self-driving car pulled up beside us at a red light, its rooftop sensors whirring like some kind of demented mechanical sombrero. I watched it cautiously edge forward, moving with all the confidence of a teenager in a driver's ed car. These autonomous vehicles were becoming an increasingly common sight, diligently learning the streets like dutiful students while I played unwitting teacher.

There was a certain irony in sharing the road with my future replacement. Here I was, part of the rideshare revolution that had disrupted traditional taxis, now watching the next wave of disruption practicing its three-point turns. The wheel of progress never stops turning—just ask the Detroit auto workers who watched robots take over assembly lines, or the switchboard operators who became obsolete overnight. We're all just cogs in the machine, each generation destined to both disrupt and be disrupted.

I found myself wondering what the old-school taxi drivers thought when they first saw us rideshare drivers cruising their streets with our fancy apps and furry mustaches. Did they feel the same mix of fascination and dread that I felt watching these self-driving cars make their tentative way through traffic? Progress, it seems, is just another way of saying "your turn's coming."

We wove through the Financial District, narrowly avoiding a collision with a scooter, I reflected on how GPS had changed the nature of my job. Gone were the days of memorizing street maps and landmarks. Now, it was all about interpreting the sometimes-questionable wisdom of satellites and algorithms.

We finally arrived at our destination, a nondescript office building that probably housed the next big tech startup. My passenger hurried off without so much as a thank-you, but I felt a twinge of pride. Despite the GPS's best efforts to lead us astray, we had made it—on time and in one piece.

I merged back into traffic, ready for my next pickup. The GPS was already calculating the route, its cheerful "ding" a reminder of our codependent relationship.

GPS has made us all idiots. Sure, it's a lifesaver when you're navigating streets with names like "Oak Ridge Avenue" and "Oak

Ridge Circle" that are somehow 12 miles apart, but there's a dark side to this convenience. We've become those people who can't find their own living room without a digital voice telling us to take a left at the coffee table. The upside? We're never truly lost, even if we've just driven 15 minutes in the wrong direction because the GPS said, "turn right" and we obeyed like sheep. The downside is that we've handed over our sense of direction to a machine that, frankly, doesn't care if we end up in a lake. There's a real joy in knowing where you are, but these days, I'm just glad if I know which way is up, and that's only if my phone's compass isn't stuck recalibrating.

I picked up my next passenger and it occurred to me that perhaps life itself was like GPS—sometimes you had to ignore the suggested route and trust your instincts. Each curve in the road seemed to trigger a fresh wave of digital anxiety from my electronic navigator, its calm voice growing increasingly strained with each deviation from its prescribed path.

I glanced at my GPS, its screen glowing with the route to my next pickup. For once, it seemed to be in perfect agreement with my intended direction. "Turn right to end your journey," it intoned.

"Not yet," I said aloud. "We've still got a few more turns to make."

CHAPTER 14

The Hangover Express

WORKING THE NIGHT SHIFT REVEALED a hidden time zone beneath San Francisco's glittering surface. Between 2 a.m. and dawn, the city transformed into a surreal alternate reality—one where the usual social boundaries blurred, and I became keeper of secrets that would die in the light of day, or at least be forgotten in next morning's hangover.

My body, fueled by a steady diet of coffee and cheese danishes, was running on fumes, much like the car I was piloting. Rounding a corner in North Beach, a sign caught my eye: "Load Limit 5 Tons." I wondered if that applied to the collective weight of questionable life choices I've encountered.

Pulling up to the bar, a beacon of grime and trendiness in equal measure, my phone let out a familiar ding. A long ride, no less than 45 minutes to Fremont. Perfect, I thought, just the fare I needed to hit my goal for the day.

About 15 minutes until destination, my passenger began a peculiar symphony of fidgeting and throat clearing.

"Excuse me," he said, his voice strained. "I, uh, I need to water the plants."

I glanced in the rearview mirror, perplexed. Plants? In my car? Then it hit me. "We are almost there," I replied hoping he could hold it.

"Pull over," he practically shouted. "Pull over right now, or I'm going to pee on your floor!"

Panic seized me as we careened down the highway at 75 miles per hour. Pee in my car? Not on my watch. I scanned the horizon for the nearest exit, praying it would come soon.

The off-ramp finally loomed, so I veered sharply onto a residential street, tires almost squealing. The man flung open the door before I'd even come to a full stop, sprinting toward the house and promptly fertilized someone's manicured lawn in Union City.

When he returned, sheepish but relieved, I regarded him with a mix of disgust and pity. "Everything okay?" I asked.

He nodded, already staring straight ahead, lost in thought. I shifted the car into drive, muttering a silent prayer that my upholstery had survived the ordeal unscathed. When we merged back onto the highway, I couldn't help but wonder—was this the price one paid for a long ride to Fremont?

These late shifts offered a masterclass in human vulnerability. The tech CEO who spent twenty minutes crying about his golden retriever's arthritis. The drag queen who gave me an impromptu makeup tutorial while changing out of her show costume. The newly engaged couple who had their first fight in my back seat over whether *Star Wars* or *Star Trek* had the better understanding of intergalactic politics.

Night driving had its own peculiar rhythm. You learned to read the city's moods like a sailor reads the sea. The wave of financial district workers at happy hour gave way to the theater crowd, then the dinner rush, then the club scene. By 3 a.m., the streets belonged to the true night dwellers—restaurant workers, club staff, security guards, and those who hadn't yet accepted that their evening was over.

Sometimes these nights took unexpected turns. Like when two cocktail competition judges climbed into my car, deeply engaged in what sounded like an Olympic-level debate about proper garnish placement and the metaphysical implications of drink presentation. Their conversation was a blend of mixology expertise and tipsy enthusiasm that only San Francisco could produce.

"Creativity is the same thing, I think. Yeah?" one of them said, his words slightly slurred.

"I'd actually give that a ten," his companion replied. "But that's high."

Their earnest discussion about "accessibility" and "wow factor" made me wonder if I'd stumbled into an alternate universe where cocktails had replaced fine art.

Then there was that surreal Monday morning when my phone pinged with what turned out to be my most sobering pickup yet. Outside a nondescript industrial building. A man stood clutching himself, his friend explaining in hushed tones that I was taking him to rehab. The weight of that responsibility sat heavy in my chest as I helped him into the car, his eyes distant, focused on a horizon only he could see.

While we drove, I couldn't help but ponder about his story. What series of events had led him to this moment? I imagined late nights filled with laughter that gradually turned hollow, mornings spent battling invisible demons, and the slow realization that he needed help. His silence spoke volumes, punctuated only by the occasional deep sigh that seemed to carry the weight of a thousand regrets.

Just as we turned onto Divisadero, I got another ping—a reminder that this was a shared ride. Soon, my car became a rolling microcosm of San Francisco—a man taking his first tentative steps toward recovery, two young female professionals, and me, the accidental ringmaster of this mobile circus.

The juxtaposition was stark—the bright-eyed enthusiasm of the young adults a stark contrast to the quiet introspection of the man headed to rehab. It was a reminder of the city's dual nature, a place of both boundless opportunity and profound struggles.

When pulled up to the rehab center, a Victorian mansion whose elegant bones still showed through its institutional conversion, I caught the eye of two staff members. They moved toward the car with practiced efficiency, knowing exactly how to shoulder the weight of someone else's rock bottom.

The day stretched on into night, each hour bringing its own brand of surreal. I picked up three medical students outside a bar in Hayes Valley, still in their hospital scrubs. They had gone for "one quick drink" after a 16-hour shift that had stretched to four cocktails and an ill-advised karaoke performance. We drove off and they debated the merits of different hospital cafeterias with the intensity usually reserved for Michelin-starred restaurants.

"UCSF's Tuesday meatloaf," one insisted, "is a transcendent culinary experience."

"You only think that because you were coming off a 20-hour shift and would have eaten a shoe," his friend countered.

The third had fallen asleep mid-argument, head resting against the window, still clutching a half-eaten bag of Flamin' Hot Cheetos.

These night shifts started feeling like an anthropological study of human behavior when the usual social filters malfunctioned. I watched first dates end before they began, friendship dynamics implode over who should have covered the last round, and countless variations of that universal 3 a.m. conversation about whether anyone actually has their life figured out.

Around 4 a.m., I picked up a group of line cooks from a closing kitchen. They piled in smelling of grease and weariness, comparing battle scars from the night's service. One proudly showed off a fresh burn on his forearm. "Table of twelve walked in five minutes before closing," he explained. "Ordered everything well-done." His colleagues nodded in solemn understanding.

The night had darker turns too. Once, I picked up three passengers heading across the Golden Gate Bridge—two women and a man riding a wave of liquid courage. No sooner had we hit the span than the back seat transformed into an impromptu love nest, the two women making out with the enthusiasm that would have impressed a romance novelist. Their male companion provided color commentary like a sportscaster at a championship game, until suddenly—WHAM!—a foot connected with the back of my head. In their alcohol-fueled acrobatics, someone had managed to kick me in the head. While I was driving. Across the Golden Gate Bridge.

Just when I thought things couldn't get more surreal, the guy decided this moment required more drama. He rolled down the window and leaned out, whooping into the night like a frat boy version of Kate Winslet in *Titanic*.

"WOOOOO!" he yelled, his voice trailing off into the fog. Which sounded like, "I AM JACK'S COMPLETE LACK OF INHIBITION!"

I watched his shadow dance across the pavement ahead, illuminated by passing lights, while contemplating how I'd explain to the Coast Guard if he decided to take a midnight swim.

In contrast, there was the night a group of middle agers from Berkeley convinced me to abandon my shift and join them at 1015 Folsom for a Paul Oakenfold set. "The ticket's worth what you'd make driving anyway," they insisted, their enthusiasm infectious. Sometimes the best rides are the ones that take you off your planned route entirely.

The city revealed itself differently in these hours. Streets I knew by heart during the day became strange and unfamiliar. Neighborhoods shifted their personalities—the Marina's carefully maintained facade cracked, the Mission's energy turned inward, Nob Hill's lights winked like distant stars as the fog rolled in.

By the time sunrise painted the bay in watercolor hues, I'd become a keeper of moments that existed outside normal time. The investment banker who confessed his secret dream of becoming a pastry chef. The bride who left her own wedding reception early because she realized she'd made a terrible mistake. The tourist who couldn't remember his hotel's name but could perfectly recall every meal he'd eaten in the city.

Dawn brought its own regulars. Early-morning airport runs, walk-of-shamers trying to look dignified, and that particular species of party-goer who insisted the night wasn't over yet, even as coffee shops began opening their doors. The city never really slept; it just shifted through different states of consciousness.

Sometimes I'd end my shift as the first joggers appeared, their fresh-faced determination a stark contrast to my passengers' smudged makeup and rumpled suits. We'd exchange nods at red lights, acknowledging each other across the divide between night and day, between those ending their stories and those just beginning.

I began to think of these night shifts as collecting fragments of people's lives—moments they might not remember but that painted a portrait of the city's true nature. In the darkness, San Francisco revealed itself as both harder and softer than its daylight persona suggested, more honest about its contradictions, more forgiving of its residents' flaws.

Perhaps that's why I kept coming back to these night shifts, even as they left me feeling like I existed slightly out of phase with normal time. In the darkness, the city's masks slipped, and for a few hours, we were all just trying to find our way home.

CHAPTER 15

The Ethical Slut's Guide to Rideshare Etiquette

MY PHONE PINGED WITH A ride request from an apartment complex. I pulled up to find a young woman, barely out of her teens, nervously clutching her purse. As she slid into the front seat, I caught a wave of perfume strong enough to qualify as a chemical weapon. "Thanks," she mumbled, eyes darting around. "I need to go to San Francisco. Is that okay?"

"Of course," I said, and we merged onto the Bay Bridge toward the city lights. She started to open up, revealing that she was on her way to meet a "client" at a hotel. It didn't take Sherlock Holmes to decode what kind of "client" she was meeting. I listened, nodding along as she shared the details of her new career path.

I thought back to some of my other rides when the back seat had been more, let's say, "interactive." Of course, that old chestnut when I got kicked in the head while driving across the Golden Gate Bridge. I'm still not sure if I should have been impressed or sought therapy. But another time I picked up a couple from a Christmas party in Mill Valley. It was late, maybe 10:15 p.m., and they were deep in the holiday spirit—and by "spirit" I mean tequila shots and poor judgment. Right after merging onto the highway, the woman disappeared below seat level, delivering her partner an early Christmas present. I cleared my throat and turned up the radio, trying to drown out Frank Sinatra's "My Way" with the sound of my own mortification.

A minute and a half later—yes, I checked the clock—he made a quiet grunt, and I was left marveling at their boldness. The back seat of a stranger's car seemed an odd place for intimacy, but I suppose when the mood strikes...

When we crossed into San Francisco, my current passenger's nerves peaked. "I'm kind of new to this," she confessed, her voice mixing excitement and anxiety. I felt a strange blend of concern and admiration for this young. I thought about the friends-turned-sex-workers I'd known over the years, their stories of empowerment and exploitation swirling in my mind like the fog over the bay.

Slipping into the role of accidental sex educator, I found myself saying, "You know, there's a great book called *The Ethical Slut* that might help. It's all about navigating nontraditional relationships, including this line of work."

She blinked at me, caught between surprise and amusement. "I never thought I'd get sex advice from my rideshare driver."

I found myself sharing safety tips, the importance of boundaries, and the value of self-respect in any relationship—sugar-coated or otherwise. By the time we pulled up to the hotel, she seemed steadier, less jittery.

"Thanks," she said as she climbed out. "Not just for the ride, but for listening. And for not judging."

I couldn't help but wonder about her future. Would she find empowerment in this work, or exploitation? Would she remember the weird rideshare driver who gave her unsolicited advice about ethical sluttery?

The moral ambiguity also hit me: Was I enabling activities of questionable legality by dropping her off? Or was I providing a safe ride to someone who would have found her way there regardless?

The night wore on, I found myself pondering the strange role I'd stumbled into: part driver, part therapist, part sex-ed instructor. It wasn't what I'd expected when I signed up for this gig, but in a city that prided itself on pushing boundaries, every ride was a peek into the evolving landscape of human desire and connection.

Eventually I understood that my steering wheel wasn't a moral compass, and my driver's seat wasn't a judge's bench. My role was simply to navigate the city's tangled streets while my passengers navigated their own complicated lives. Some were writing their stories in neon, others in invisible ink, but none of them needed my permission to live them.

CHAPTER 16

The Crosswalk Chronicles

IF THERE'S ANOTHER THING SAN Francisco excels at, it's juxtaposition. Where else can you find a twenty-something tech billionaire stepping over a sleeping homeless person on their way to buy a $15 avocado toast? The city is a constant reminder that life rarely fits into neat categories, much like the ever-changing rules of its crosswalks.

I was pondering this as I drove through the Financial District's morning rush. The fog was just starting to lift, revealing glimpses of steel and glass towers stretching toward a stubbornly gray sky.

My passenger, a woman with a severe bob and an even more severe expression, was engrossed in her phone, likely firing off emails before her 9 a.m. meeting. I'd picked her up from one of those sleek high-rises in SoMa, the kind that probably had a meditation room and an organic juice bar in the lobby.

Right as we approached a crosswalk, a group of tourists stepped out into the street, blissfully unaware of the "Don't Walk" sign flashing its angry red hand. I slammed on the brakes, sending my passenger lurching forward, her phone flying under the seat.

"Jesus Christ!" she exclaimed, her carefully curated professional demeanor cracking like her phone screen. "Don't these people know how to read?"

I bit back a chuckle. In my experience, crosswalks in San Francisco were more like suggestions than actual rules. I'd seen people sprint across six lanes of traffic on Van Ness, dodging cars like it was an extreme sport. And the cyclists—they seemed to think traffic lights were purely decorative.

While my passenger fumbled for her phone, muttering curses that would make a sailor blush, I reflected on the crosswalks of life. How many times had I ignored the flashing "Don't Walk" signs in my own journey? Taking this job, for instance, was definitely a case of jaywalking across the career highway.

We inched forward as the tourists finally made it across, waving apologetically. The light turned green, but before I could accelerate, a man pushing a shopping cart piled high with what looked like the entire inventory of a defunct RadioShack stepped into the crosswalk.

My passenger let out a groan that seemed to come from the depths of her soul. We waited, I noticed the stark contrast between him and the shiny tech workers scurrying past, AirPods in ears, eyes glued to screens. It was like watching two different worlds collide at the crosswalk, neither acknowledging the other's existence.

Suddenly, a food delivery robot zipped across our path, its little flag waving jauntily as it navigated the crosswalk with more confidence than most humans. "What the hell was that?" my passenger exclaimed, momentarily forgetting her lost phone.

"Welcome to San Francisco," I replied, "where even the robots have better street smarts than the tourists."

We neared her destination; my passenger finally spoke again. "I've lived here for ten years," she said, more to herself than to me, "and sometimes I still feel like I'm crossing against the grain."

I nodded, understanding completely. "I think that's just San Francisco," I replied. "The city where everyone's a jaywalker in their own way."

She let out a small laugh as we pulled up to her destination. For the first time since she'd entered the car, I saw her smile.

I watched her disappear into the stream of morning commuters, her heels clicking against concrete as she merged with the Financial District's relentless current. San Francisco's crosswalks tell more truth about the city than any tourism brochure ever could. Here, venture capitalists in North Face vests share curb space with artists in paint-splattered jeans. Tech workers on electric scooters weave between people taking their dogs for a walk, while tourists clutch their phones like talismans, trying to decode street signs that even locals find cryptic.

Each intersection writes its own story in the pauses between green lights. A man pushing a shopping cart filled with aluminum cans waits beside a woman carrying a thousand-dollar yoga mat. Neither looks at the other, but for these few moments, they share the same slice of sidewalk, breathe the same fog-filtered air. The light changes, and their worlds separate again.

My job was to witness these brief convergences, these moments when San Francisco's carefully constructed social barriers dissolved at the painted lines of a crosswalk. To watch the city's different realities bump against each other like currents in the bay, mixing briefly before flowing apart again.

The next light turned red, and I eased to a stop. Ahead of me, a group of software engineers discussed their latest app while a street poet shouted verses about the death of the American Dream. Neither seemed aware of the other, yet here they were, sharing the same moment, the same corner, the same city. Sometimes I think that's all San Francisco really is—a collection of worlds that were never meant to meet, somehow finding themselves waiting for the same light to change.

CHAPTER 17

Last Ride

THE "END ROAD WORK" SIGN seemed fitting for the last chapter of this book. After 4,615 rides, countless hours behind the wheel, and more stories than a library of misfit tales, my journey as a rideshare driver was supposedly coming to an end. Or so I thought.

The truth was, I'd landed another corporate job, trading my rental car keys for a keycard to yet another glass tower full of ergonomic chairs and free snacks. After two years of freedom on the road, I was willingly re-entering the fluorescent-lit cage of conference calls and casual Fridays. The irony wasn't lost on me—I'd escaped one corporate job only to seek refuge in another. But at least this time I had better stories to share at the water cooler.

It was a typically atypical San Francisco day—the kind when you need sunglasses, an umbrella, and a parka all within the span of an hour. I'd just dropped off my last official passenger, a sleep-deprived ER doctor heading home after a shift that made my longest days look like a catnap.

He stumbled out of the car and mumbled something about the music being nice. "Thanks for the ride," he said. "Nice to end a tough shift on a beautiful note." I watched him shuffle toward his building, wondering if he'd even remember our ride once he woke up.

I merged back into traffic, memories flooded my mind, each passenger a unique piece in the unusual mosaic of my rideshare career. There was the woman heading to divorce court, her story of heartbreak unfolding as we crossed the Bay Bridge. The young sex worker I'd dropped off at that hotel months ago—I'd often wondered if my unsolicited advice about *The Ethical Slut* had helped her navigate her new career. Or had she moved on to less controversial pursuits, such as disrupting the avocado toast industry or inventing the next unnecessary app?

I remembered the group of drag queens who'd turned my car into a mobile disco as we cruised down Market Street. For weeks after, I'd found glitter in crevices of the car I didn't even know existed. Then there were the tech bros and their heated debates about their latest world-changing app ideas. I still couldn't decide if "Kombucha Wine" or "Tinder for Cats" was the most ridiculous concept I'd heard.

I'd played more roles than I could count—therapist, career counselor, amateur sex educator. The nights I'd been a mobile party bus, and the mornings I'd been a silent sanctuary for the hungover masses. The 4 a.m. airport runs when my passengers were sleepwalking zombies, the midday rush hour crawls when I aged a year for every block we moved.

I recalled the couple I'd picked up from the airport, returning from their fiftieth anniversary trip. They'd requested Billie Holiday, and as "I'll Be Seeing You" filled the car, they held hands in the back seat, lost in memories. I'd felt like both a time traveler and a voyeur, witnessing a love that had weathered half a century.

I thought about the ten different rental cars I'd driven, each with its own quirks and personality. The Chevy Trax with its questionable brakes that made every stop an adventure. The Ford Focus that seemed held together by hope and duct tape. The Hyundai Sonata with its impressive sound system that made every ride feel like a musical journey.

And then there was my tumultuous relationship with the GPS. Oh, how we'd battled over the years! Its insistence on sending me down one-way streets the wrong way, its stubborn belief that I could make impossible U-turns, its occasional decision to simply give up and declare "You have arrived" in the middle of nowhere.

While I cruised down the 101, familiar sights rolling by like a well-worn film reel, I realized that this job had given me more than just a paycheck and an intimate knowledge of every public restroom in the Bay Area. It had given me a front-row seat to the human comedy, a crash course in empathy, and a deeper understanding of the city I called home.

The "End Road Work" sign flashed by, and I couldn't help but chuckle at the irony. In San Francisco, the roadwork never really ends. The city is in a constant state of reinvention, much like its inhabitants. And maybe, I realized, so was I.

Just as I was waxing poetic about endings, my phone pinged with a new ride request. I stared at it, wondering if this was some sort of cosmic joke. For a moment, I contemplated ignoring it. After all, this was supposed to be my grand finale. But then I thought about all the unexpected turns this job had taken me on, all the stories that had unfolded in my back seat.

With a mixture of resignation and excitement, I accepted the ride. When I pulled up to the pickup location, I couldn't help but laugh. There, waiting on the curb, was a man dressed as a giant avocado.

"You're my ride?" the avocado asked, his voice muffled by the costume.

"Apparently," I replied. "Where to?"

"Downtown. I'm a social media influencer for a health food company. We're doing a guerrilla marketing campaign."

As I helped him extract his oversized green body out of the car, he turned to me with a grin. "You know, you should write a book about all this. I bet it would be hilarious."

I watched him waddle away, a green beacon of weirdness in a sea of ordinary. And just like that, I knew. This wasn't really the end of my journey. It was just the beginning of a new chapter.

I glanced at my GPS, its screen glowing with the route to the rental car return lot. For one last time, it seemed to be in perfect agreement with my intended direction. "In five hundred feet, turn right to end your journey," it intoned, its robotic voice almost wistful.

"Not yet," I said aloud. "We've still got a few more turns to make."

Reflections on the Road

While writing this, I couldn't help but marvel at the unexpected journey that brought me here. What started as a way to make ends meet became a master class in human nature, a crash course in urban anthropology, and a journey of self-discovery that I never saw coming.

Looking back, I realize that my time behind the wheel was more than just a job—it was a transformative experience that reshaped my understanding of the world and my place in it. Here are some of the most profound lessons I learned along the way:

1. **Empathy is a Superpower**: In the confined space of a car, I encountered people from all walks of life, each carrying their own hopes, fears, and stories. I learned to read the subtle cues—a sigh, a nervous tap of the fingers, a faraway look—and adjust my approach accordingly. Sometimes, all a person needed was a listening ear, and other times, they craved the comfort of silence. This heightened empathy hasn't just made me a better driver, but a better human being.

2. **Judgment is a Rearview Mirror**: I picked up CEOs and homeless individuals, brides on their wedding day and people fresh out of jail. Each ride taught me that first impressions are often misleading, and that everyone has depth and complexity beyond what meets the eye. I learned to suspend judgment and approach each interaction with an open mind and heart.

3. **Adaptability is Key**: From navigating ever-changing traffic patterns to dealing with last-minute route changes and passenger mood swings, I learned to roll with the punches. This flexibility

has served me well beyond my driving days, helping me navigate life's unexpected turns with grace and humor.

4. **The City is a Living Entity**: Driving through San Francisco's diverse neighborhoods at all hours of the day and night gave me an intimate understanding of the city's rhythms and moods. I witnessed the city wake up, go to sleep, celebrate, and mourn. This deep connection to my urban environment has given me a sense of belonging I never knew I was missing.

5. **Every Interaction is an Opportunity**: Whether it was a five-minute ride or an hour-long journey, I learned that every interaction held the potential for connection, learning, or a great story. This mindset has enriched my life immeasurably, turning even mundane encounters into opportunities for growth and understanding.

6. **Humor is the Best Navigation System**: When faced with difficult passengers, impossible traffic, or absurd situations (like helping an avocado-costumed man into my car), I found that humor was often the best way to diffuse tension and make the journey enjoyable for everyone involved. This ability to find the funny in the frustrating has become a vital life skill.

7. **Resilience Comes from Small Victories**: On days when the tips were low and the traffic was high, I learned to celebrate small wins—a genuine thank you from a passenger, navigating a tricky intersection smoothly, or finding the perfect song for the moment. This focus on small joys has helped me build resilience in all areas of my life.

8. **Everyone Has a Story Worth Hearing**: From the seemingly mundane to the wildly extraordinary, I discovered that every passenger had a unique tale to tell. This realization has made me more curious about the people around me and more appreciative of the diversity of human experience.

9. **The Journey is as Important as the Destination**: While my job was to get people from point A to point B, I learned that the ride itself could be just as significant as the arrival. This perspective has helped me appreciate life's in-between moments and find meaning in the process, not just the outcome.
10. **Self-Reflection is a Two-Way Street**: As much as I observed and learned about others, I also gained profound insights about myself. The solitude of empty rides and the intensity of full ones provided ample opportunity for introspection, helping me understand my own motivations, fears, and aspirations.

If there's one thing that driving rideshare taught me, it's that entitlement knows no bounds. I've had passengers of all ages, races, and socioeconomic backgrounds treat me with a level of disdain that would make even the most jaded customer service veteran blush. But for every rude encounter, there were countless more moments of connection, laughter, and shared humanity. In the end, I learned not to take the entitled behavior personally—it reflected them and not me.

While I transition from driver to writer, I carry these lessons with me like precious cargo. They've not only shaped the stories I want to tell but have fundamentally altered how I view the world and my place in it. My time as a rideshare driver may have come to an end, but the journey of growth and discovery it set me on is far from over.

In many ways, writing this book feels like embarking on a new ride—destination unknown, but full of possibility. And just like in my driving days, I'm buckling up, turning on the ignition, and preparing for whatever adventures lie ahead. Because if there's one thing I've learned, it's that life, like San Francisco traffic, is full of surprising turns, unexpected detours, and beautiful views just around the corner.

So here's to the road ahead, to the stories yet to be told, and to all the passengers—past, present, and future—who make the journey worthwhile. May your rides be smooth, your conversations enlightening, and your destinations worth the trip. And remember, in the grand rideshare of life, we're all just trying to get somewhere— might as well enjoy the ride.